To: Dave & Janel
From:

# Petals
## — OF THE —
# Heart

Keyoka Rock

*Enjoy,*
*Keyoka*

ISBN 978-1-63903-687-5 (paperback)
ISBN 978-1-63903-688-2 (digital)

Copyright © 2023 by Keyoka Rock

All rights reserved. No part of this publication may be reproduced, distributed, or transmitted in any form or by any means, including photocopying, recording, or other electronic or mechanical methods without the prior written permission of the publisher. For permission requests, solicit the publisher via the address below.

Christian Faith Publishing
832 Park Avenue
Meadville, PA 16335
www.christianfaithpublishing.com

Printed in the United States of America

In memory of Pastor C. R. Johnson and Bishop James F. Copeland of Brooklyn Tabernacle Deliverance Center. I will never forget the preached Word of God, in which you have labored and shared. Because of your obedience to the call to preach God's Word, I have become an Anointed Ambassador for Christ.

    In memory of my dad, Albert Nicholas. Your unexpected passing in 2020 was devastating. I wish we had more time together. You are gone too soon but will not be forgotten. You are love and will be missed.

To my lovely mother, Rhonda Rock. I thank God for you. Your faith in God has empowered me. Your encouraging words have molded me. Your continued love has pushed me to soar into my destiny. I love you. I appreciate you. I thank you for being the wonderful mother that you are!

# Contents

Foreword ..................................................................................9
Preface ...................................................................................11
Acknowledgments ...............................................................13
Testimony .............................................................................15
1: Blessed to See Another Birthday ....................................19
2: Writing: The Gift That Brings Peace .............................21
3: I Trust in the Lord .........................................................23
4: The Source Behind That Issue .......................................24
5: I Fell, but God Picked Me Up! ......................................26
6: Spiritual Sacrifice: A Desperate Fight to Live! ...............30
7: Faith Walk .....................................................................34
8: It's Just a Shadow ..........................................................35
9: Everything Is Going to Be All Right .............................38
10: Vessel of Praise ...............................................................41
11: Bended Knee Victories ...................................................42
12: Prayer of Distress Births Strength and Victory! .............44
13: The Unprofitable Enemy ................................................48
14: The Inferno ....................................................................50
15: Anointing Activated .......................................................52
16: Saints of God, Pick Up Your Weapons! ........................53
17: The Fight Is On! ............................................................56
18: Satan, You're Going Down! ...........................................56
19: God + Issue = Solved ....................................................59
20: Just a Test ......................................................................60
21: An "In Spite of" Praise ..................................................62
22: Tasted Jesus Yet? ............................................................63
23: A Love above the Rest ...................................................64
24: God's Plan of Redemption ............................................66
25: Choose This Day Who You Will Serve .........................67

# Foreword

Whether she is singing praises to God, directing the church choir, or delivering powerful poetic art, Keyoka Rock seeks to empower and win souls for the kingdom of God.

*Petals of the Heart* is an anointed work of art that stems from the innermost depth of the author's soul. It is a testimony of the obstacles, trials, victories, and miracles in this ambassador's life. Ms. Rock delicately plucks petals from the flower blossoms in her heart to express her passion for Christ and to encourage others to use their lives and gifts to glorify God.

This book is a true manifestation of God. It will cause strongholds to be broken, deliverance to those spiritually captive, and restoration to the ailing soul; this book is sure to empower both believers and nonbelievers alike. The testimony and life-changing poetry displayed in this book will compel you to pick up your swords and fight for everything the devil has stolen from you. "Satan, You're Going Down" is just one of the many *Petals of the Heart* that will give you the strength to fight.

I assure you that this book will meet you on your journey as you quest for meaning, hope, and empowerment. The truth displayed in this book will help you uncover and/or strengthen your greatness, your potential, and your purpose in God's kingdom. Because of the author's transparency and passion, this book is surely a page-turner.

The spiritual faith walk which this ambassador for Christ, Keyoka Rock, avows to live is a message that is relatable and one which will empower you. It is a story that should be proclaimed to all. *Petals of the Heart* is an opportunity to experience poetic art and Christianity at its best.

Latasha S. Butler,<br>
Author of *A Sista Speaks*

# Preface

*Petals of the Heart* is a book of simple, yet revelatory, poetic expressions. These stem from my innermost thoughts and feelings that ruptured as a result of periods of trial as well as periods of victory in my life.

The "Testimony" rendered is my acknowledgment to God presented as a short story. This short story depicts a special moment in my childhood in which I was reminded of how great, powerful, merciful, limitless, and, to sum it up, how all mighty God is!

This *testimony*, along with the revelatory poems within this book, will encourage those experiencing similar circumstances that every hindrance, sickness, disorder, and diabolical force, raging war against you, can be annihilated through the power of God; for God is more than able to deliver, heal, protect, restore, save, and empower you!

This book is sure to strengthen and motivate believers, in Jesus the Christ, to walk in their God-given authority and combat every negative force whether natural or spiritual. Through prayer, faith, and speaking the Word of God, you can live a victorious life!

# Acknowledgments

I would like to recognize my mother, Rhonda Rock, my grandmother Betty (affectionately known as Betty-Boo), my brother Al, my aunt Denise, aunt Lisa, aunt Debbie, aunt Mimi, aunt Sherrie, uncle Eddie, granddad Rock, grandpa Nicholas, my cousins, and friends. You have all supported me in various ways which helped fuel the momentum needed for completing this book—whether through words of affirmation, giving me a platform to recite my poetry, challenging me to persevere while working on this project, or just believing in my ability to accomplish my goals. Thank you all for encouraging me through the process of completing this project. Your excitement for this book has been breathtaking. And to Latasha Butler, you're the best! Thanks for your input. Your kind words are heartfelt. To Apostle Agnes Jones, of Almost Midnight Ministries, thank you for affording me the platform to render my poetry. Your prayers and contribution to this project are much valued and have been such an encouragement to me. Also to my spiritual mother, Christina Cain, whom I've crowned as my dear Mama T, words can't express how much I cherish you. Your insight, wisdom, and warnings to stay prayerful and be led by the Lord have helped me continue to stay focused on God's plan. I am forever grateful to you for your prayers and support. And last but not least, to Jerry Childs, thank you for affording me the opportunity to render my poetry at the Brownsville Recreational Center. I am forever grateful to you!

Thank you all for being such a great encouragement to me. I am blessed to have you all in my life! May God abundantly bless you!

# Testimony

"Precious, do you know you are a walking miracle?" my mom said to me while we were in the kitchen of our Brooklyn, New York, apartment. I must have been around the age of ten and had come home from school, feeling discouraged about my life again. My mom was always prepared to edify me and did not hesitate to remind me of my *miracle child* status.

"You are blessed, and—"

"But, Mom," I said, cutting her off, knowing she was about to go into the story of how I am a recipient of miracles. Wanting to vent, I whined. "Mom, why do I have to stay in special ed? I do well on all my tests! I want to attend general ed. classes now!"

"Sweetheart," my mom would say, "you're doing an excellent job in school! You're receiving special education as a result of the health issues you endured, and the care you needed caused you to miss out on school for quite some time, so your doctors and I believe special ed will help you to catch up and become even stronger with your learning. General education may be a little too fast-paced for you right now. Precious, do you remember when you were sick?"

"I remember some things, Mom," I responded. I listened intensely as she told the story of testimonies that I was too young to fully remember but could never really forget.

"You went through some traumatic life-threatening periods in your young life. I remember when you were around three years old, and you took hold of and swallowed several prescription pills and had to get your stomach pumped. Precious, I was so scared. I didn't know what to do. All I knew to do was pray that the doctors would save your life, and God answered my prayer! From that day forward,

I knew God was real. I was so happy to have you back home healthy, strong, and growing up beautifully.

"But just two years later, your health took a turn for the worst, which was a result of an unfortunate choking incident that occurred while you were eating dinner one night. Paramedics came to care for you and proceeded to clear your windpipe but couldn't find what was blocking it. You became unconscious while being transported to the hospital.

"While at the hospital, you were slipping in and out of consciousness and beginning to suffer from reoccurring seizures. Doctors couldn't determine what was causing the seizures. They ruled out the choking incident because you were now breathing on your own. However, the seizures progressed until your ability to see, talk, and walk was fully diminished, and you slipped into a coma.

"Doctors thought you were going to die and suggested that I allow them to insert a feeding tube into your stomach. They said this would help to save your life, but the feeding tube could never be removed. Sweetie, I didn't want you to have this tube stuck in you for the rest of your life, so I didn't allow them to perform the procedure, and then a few months went by, and you were still in a coma.

"One day, while attending a church service at the Brooklyn Tabernacle Deliverance Center, I stood on the prayer request line and asked the pastor to pray that God would heal your body and take you out of the comatose state you were in. Not only did he pray, but the ministers and the mothers of the church began visiting you at the hospital, and each time they came, they would anoint your body with oil while petitioning God to heal you completely.

"Now seven months into this comatose state, I sat at your bedside, as I routinely did, talking to you, reading to you, and praying for a miracle. I didn't realize that somewhere in the midst of me talking, you had woken up out of the coma and were now looking at me. I watched in shock as you began looking around the room. Then I embraced you so tightly and asked, 'Precious, where were you all that time?'

"And you answered me! You said, 'I was sitting on Jesus's lap, Mommy.'

"I was just stuck in amazement, and I could only watch on as you began removing tubes from your arms and nose. Then you proceeded to get up out of the bed. I followed you out of the hospital room, down the hallway, and into the room where you saw kids eating and watching television. I rushed to get the doctors so they could witness the *miracle*! You had come out of the coma!

"When I returned to the room with the doctors, you had been grabbing food from the kids and eating it. When I began to stop you, the doctors said, 'No, Ms. Rock, let her eat!'

"That very day, the doctors released you from the hospital. You didn't have to come home with any medications, and you didn't have any more seizures. God healed you completely!

"Sweetheart, let this testimony of your life remind you of how blessed you are. Never forget what God has done for you. God has his hands on you. You are a walking miracle, a child of God, and you are blessed.

"Precious, God has blessed you to be one of the top students in your class. If you want to move from special education to general education, all you have to do is pray and ask God to help you advance.

"And guess what!"

"What?" I replied.

"He will! But you must continue studying hard, and you should continue to help teach the kids in your class how to do the assignments, and God will bless you, okay?"

"Okay, Mom," I responded with eagerness.

I followed my mother's instructions. *That same year*, I graduated from Public School 332 as an elected valedictorian and received countless certificates and awards, which included, but were not limited to, a savings bond as well as a plaque for teaching. I was transferred from special education to general education, which I was to begin in junior high school.

I learned at an early age about God and what He is able to do. I would not only receive constant reminders from my mom and my family, but as I've gotten older, I have also received reminders from those who knew my mom during that time when I had been sick.

They wouldn't hesitate to stop me, when we crossed paths in the street, just to tell me how they knew what God had done for me. The conversation has always started off with the question, "You're Rhonda Rock's daughter, aren't you? Girl, you may not remember me, but I remember when you were sick! You are a walking miracle!"

As they would look at me in amazement, I have always smiled and replied, "God is good!"

Until this day, God has never ceased to amaze me! He has blessed me in every area of my life both spiritually and naturally. My life is not my own, but it belongs to God. I appreciate and honor Jesus as my savior, healer, deliverer, father, friend, provider, and so much more, but most of all, He is my King. He is the Lord over my life, and I give Him all glory for all things big and small, which He has done and for everything He has yet to manifest in my life.

# Blessed to See Another Birthday

Lord, you let me see another beautiful day.
The birds are singing.
Sunrays are beaming through clouds above.
Streaks of purple dress the pale blue sky.
Cottony clouds trail those blazing orange,
As they float by; so beautiful the colors are—
Depictions of how artistic you are.

Such a wonderful day you've allowed me to see
And experience more of your grace and mercies
On this November 21, 2002
Not just another day, but my Birthday too.
I give you praise for you have given me—
Another day, doctors never thought I would see.

They thought I would have died, but
You allowed them to see
Your mighty hands reconstruct me.
Your *ruach* breath took over my being.
And on the seventh month of my comatose state
You resurrected me.

The number seven—
The number of completion.
You created me a body free from sickness.

*Keyoka Rock*

Restored all of my senses—
You rebuked deafness and
Blindness too.
Lameness had to go because you told it to!
Lord, you chose me before I entered my mother's womb—
Created me to be an ambassador for you.
When I became old enough to understand
The magnificent God you are,
I confessed you to be my Savior, my God,
My Bright and Morning Star.
Years later, I'm still claiming you to be
The True and Living God…my Everything!
Lord, I promise each day you allow me to live
To become a better servant for you, oh God—
My Redeemer, my Strength
My Healer, my Restorer
My Father, my Peace—
My *Everything*!

# Writing: The Gift That Brings Peace

I write when I am happy
And times when I feel sad.
I write when the devil is on my track
Or when there's a test I can't seem to pass.

I write as a form of praise to God.
I write until I break free—from situations
Suppressing me.

I write to give God glory.
I write to give God praise.
I write, for it's a gift from God—
A weapon to overcome my pain.

I write, for it gives me peace and strength.
I write when I can't pray
For I know, if I can't mumble a sound
God senses my soul's thoughts, through
Words spilled out on page.

I write my testimonies
And failures I've endured.
I write my victories to remind myself
There is no situation I cannot overcome.

*Keyoka Rock*

I write to give God glory,
For He deserves my praise.
I write because it's another tool
I can use to bless His name.

# I Trust in the Lord

I hope;
I pray.
I know God will deliver
Me from my pain.

I seek;
I knock.
I speak into the air.
My words reach God's tender ears.

God hears my cry;
He sees my need.
He begins working on a remedy;
He turns my pain into victory!

God gives me strength and wisdom;
He empowers me with his might.
I also use the Word of God
To send the enemy to flight!

Out of my mouth flows praises to my King.
The master and ruler of everything.
For I know there is nothing
Too hard for God to do,
And that no matter the season,
God will see me through!

# The Source Behind That Issue

Revelations 12:9–10 (NIV)

> And the great dragon was cast out, that old serpent, called the Devil, and Satan, which deceives the whole world: he was cast out into the earth, and his angels were cast out with him. And I heard a loud voice saying in heaven, Now is come salvation, and strength, and the kingdom of our God, and the power of his Christ: for the accuser of our brethren is cast down, which accused them before our God day and night.

1 Peter 5:8–10 (KJV amplified)

> Be well balanced [temperate, sober of mind], be vigilant and cautious at all times; for that enemy of yours, the devil, roams around like a lion roaring [in fierce hunger], seeking someone to seize upon and devour. Withstand him; be firm in faith [against his onset—rooted, established, strong, immovable, and determined], knowing that the same [identical] sufferings are appointed to your brotherhood [the whole body of Christians] throughout the world. And after you have suffered a little while, the God of

all grace [Who imparts all blessing and favor], Who has called you to his [own] eternal glory in Christ Jesus, will Himself complete and make you what you ought to be, establish and ground you securely, and strengthen, and settle you.

# I Fell, but God Picked Me Up!

I fell.
The devil thought he had me.
But he might as well
Go back to hell,
For I know in whom I can tell
All of my faults and the times I rebelled.

Against God only did I commit my sins.
He gave me the power to dust myself off
And try again.

I fell, but got backup!
My rightful place with God
Is where I strive to be.
It's through God that I have victory
Against the enemy of my soul.

That evil devil
Awakes the desires of my flesh,
Tempting me to sin.
He thinks that when I fall,
The battle is over, and that he wins.

Sometimes I fall prey
To his evil devices.

My mind, body, and soul feel
Trapped—
Like a puppet on strings.
I begin to do the very things
I say I will not do.
I end up going back on my word
Fulfilling the lust of my flesh.

My flesh and my spirit are at war.
My spirit longs for God,
But in this trap,
My flesh goes against
The will of God even more.

I begin to slip;
I begin to fall.
The devil laughs at me
And turns the heat up
More…and…more.

It seems like I will never
Break through
Or pass this test!

Sensing my weakness and
Desiring to turn God's word void,
The devil seeks to steal, to kill, and to destroy.

The life—the treasures God gave to me
Are now distorted by Satan's trickery—his
Enticing passions ignite my flesh,
Knowing at times I won't digress.

*Keyoka Rock*

But even in my weakness,
I am made strong
Through God, in whom my soul belongs
And for whom my soul longs.

God won't put on me
More than I can bear.
And when the devil thinks he's winning,
God will draw near.
He rebukes the devil long enough
For me to come to my senses, and
While on bended knees,
I cry out, Lord, please
Forgive me,
Cleanse me,
Wash me,
Strengthen me.
Keep me from falling again.
I don't want to commit the same sins
Over…and…over again.

God answers my prayer.
He restores my soul,
Purifies and makes me whole.

I put on the whole armor of God
So I will be able to withstand.
I have my loins gird about with truth,
The breastplate of righteousness—
My feet shod with the preparation of
The gospel of peace.

I have on the shield of faith
So that I may quench all
The fiery darts of the wicked.
I wear the helmet of salvation

And bear the sword of the Spirit
Which is the Word of God.

Devil, you thought that you would win,
But my God has made you a liar
Yet again!
Devil, don't you know?
Can't you see?
The Almighty God—
He's protecting me!

God has a plan for my life.
Devil, you're fighting me
Because you see it,
But, because God is the greatest power
I shall not be defeated!

# Spiritual Sacrifice: A Desperate Fight to Live!

I still have the victory in spite of what I've done.
The battle for my life, Christ already won.
I have the victory, although I sinned just the other day.
I humbled myself before God and prayed,
Asking Him to forgive me
For sins committed unknowingly as well as
For those done willingly—sometimes premeditated.
Starts in the mind then manifests through actions,
But God's power won't allow my flesh to keep me backslidden.

I'm determined to live this life
So that I can live again,
Because when Christ comes back,
I want to reside with Him.

I'm determined to win,
But there's a war going on.
The fight—
My flesh against my spirit.
Let the best within me win.

Filled with the Holy Spirit
But found myself slipping.
Yes, slipping back into the pleasures of sin again.
Why would I go backwards,

While deliverance and blessings,
God continues rendering?

The infiltration of the desires of the flesh
Bring forth tests, which at times I don't pass.
Feeling like a queen in a muddy pigpen,
Upset about what I've done in the past.

Refusing to stay in this grungy state,
I gave my issues to the Father,
Who in the midst of the confusion
Regulated my mind, made me whole,
Washed me clean, restored my soul.

This Christian walk is
A continuous spiritual sacrifice.
I fight this spiritual battle
Both day and night.

God's power made me free,
But I'm still wrapped in this flesh.
Like Apostle Paul
My spirit desires to do right,
But evil surrounds me day and night.

Things the enemy can't get me to
Submit to while I'm awake are
Injected into my dreams at night.
Waking up in a cold sweat,
My flesh goes crazy.
Can't scream out the name of Jesus—because
Evil spirits are gagging me.

I refuse to allow the enemy to win,
So in the channels of my mind,
I petition God to remove Satan's grip.

*Keyoka Rock*

Shaken, but I'm set free.
My spiritual eyes watch demonic forces flee!
No longer gagged, I began to speak.

Keep your hands off of me, Satan!
I don't belong to you!
You've been messing with me
Long enough; now I'm coming after
You and your diabolical crew!

Protected by God's power.
Empowered by God's might.
Defeating the enemy
Is the focal point of my fight!

I'm going after the enemy through my witness
Winning souls for Christ, my vengeance!
Snatching souls out of Satan's grip so
They won't receive his death sentence.

Preaching and teaching the good news,
Leaving none behind, if possible.
Sharing how salvation is available—
To those who will only just believe
That no matter what they've done,
The Son of God came to set them free!

Free from bondage,
Free from sin,
Free to live,
Free to reign with him.

Life in Jesus,
A spiritual sacrifice,
A desperate fight
Against eternal demise.

Thanks be to God;
Jesus already paid the price.
It's through his triumph
We can live a triumphant life!

# Faith Walk

2 Corinthians 5:7 (KJV amplified)

> For we walk by faith [we regulate our lives and conduct ourselves by our conviction or belief, respecting man's relationship to God and divine things, with trust and holy fervor; thus, we walk] not by sight or appearance.

# It's Just a Shadow

As I walk through the valley
Of the shadow of death
The Lord is my shepherd
He guards my steps
I will fear no evil—
*It's just a shadow.*

When the pressures of this world
Try to hold me down
And all I can see
Is this shadow around,
It tries to bring death to my spirit;
It tries to bring stress to my mind.
Sometimes this pressure floods my mind.
My head begins to ache, and I feel like crying, but—
*It's just a shadow.*

When the things I did wrong constantly
Torment me,
When I fight with all my might, and
It seems I can't break free—
*It's just a shadow.*

When I look around and all things are
Going wrong,
When everything I touch seems to
Crumble and fall—
*It's just a shadow.*

*Keyoka Rock*

When fear comes over me
And I can't catch my breath
Because the shadow is so close
It seems like death is coming next—
*It's just a shadow.*

Suddenly, a moment of truth!
A *shadow* can't be seen unless
There's a reflection of light,
The prince of darkness
Surrounding me means
The Son of God is near,
Though not in natural sight.

Indicating I'm in the vicinity
Of blessings the enemy does not
Want me to obtain, but
In spite of the chaos Satan brings,
Christ endows me with tranquility
Along with revelation of the
Enemy's scheme.

Through glimpses of my path
To righteousness and eternal life,
Christ exposes the enemy's plan
To cloud my way,
To destroy my life—but
I send a message to the enemy:
I have been brought with a valuable price!
Jesus paid the price for me
Through His sacrificial life!

So, Satan, nothing you do will hinder me
From receiving what belongs to me.
None of your tactics will stop me
From becoming who God ordained me to be, because
I will continue to follow the Good Shepherd's lead
Toward my destiny!

# Everything Is Going to Be All Right

I have a feeling that everything is going to be all right.
I don't know what tomorrow will bring,
But I know God is on my side.
Sometimes life hurts,
And sometimes life is just fine.

Pushing closer to my destiny,
Trusting the Lord
To show me things
I can't naturally see—
A process that feels uncomfortable to me.

Unsure of God's will
Or which way I should go,
Trusting somehow I'll find my way, while
Traveling the narrow road
With a heart aching to live right, and
Flesh desiring the broad way to go.

I invoke the Holy Spirit to take control, so I won't lose sight.
I have a feeling everything is going to be all right.
My lamp is lit bright.
My soul is overflowing with the oil
Of God's anointing.
I refuse to miss the coming of the Lord,

So my oil I can't share with the unwise.
I can't take anyone along this ride,
Who might cause my demise!

I'd rather ride alone,
Temple filled with holy oil.
I'm driving straight to God's throne—
The throne of grace,
Where justification is shown.
Transformed—

Like the prodigal son,
I came back to my senses.
No longer banking on
Pleasures of iniquities, or
Paying wages toward the death
The enemy set out for me.

When with the price—
The sacrificial life of Jesus.
God, you redeemed me!
That I might not reap eternal damnation
But the eternal life you promised me.

Now on the right path,
Trying to live righteously
That I might receive the prophecies
You spoke to me.
Your word can't turn back to you void,
But it shall spring up!
It shall live!
It will not be destroyed!

Lord, before you created me,
Your thoughts completed me.
I was made whole before your hands formed me.

*Keyoka Rock*

Into a living being, your Word called me.
I am who I am because you molded me.

Determined to live this life
So I can live again,
My desire is to bask in your glorious presence
Without end—
So I present my body, a living sacrifice.
*Holy*—
For it's you, Lord
I want to represent.

Seeking you for who you are,
Not just for the blessings you can give.
Learning who I am in you, so a victorious life
I can live.

I travel the narrow road
Knowing
Everything is going to be *all right*!

# Vessel of Praise

God, you are my King!
Your love toward me
Causes me to sing
Praises to your name.
Let it ring!
Loud!
Cheerful!
Joyous!
Let the praises be!

Lord, you mean
So much to me.
My soul to you
Lord, I bring.

Only you can shape and
Mold me to be
The woman of God
You called me to be.
So, Lord, I submit
To your purpose for me.
And to you, oh Lord,
All glory will be!
Amen

# Bended Knee Victories

Ephesians 6:12 (KJV)

> For, we wrestle not against flesh and blood, but against principalities, against powers, against the rulers of the darkness of this world, against spiritual wickedness in high places.

Psalms 18:6 (NIV)

> In my distress I called to the Lord; I cried to my God for help. From his temple he heard my voice; my cry came before him into his ears.

Psalms 20:6 (NIV)

> Now I know that the Lord saves his anointed; he answers him from his holy heaven with the saving power of his right hand.

Luke 10:19 (KJV)

> Behold, I give unto you power to tread on serpents and scorpions, and over all the power of the enemy: and nothing shall by any means hurt you.

Matthew 16:19 (KJV amplified)

> I will give you the keys of the kingdom of heaven; and whatever you bind (declare to be improper and unlawful) on earth must be what is already bound in heaven; and whatever you loose (declare lawful) on earth must be what is already loosed in heaven.

# Prayer of Distress Births Strength and Victory!

What's going to happen to me?
Will the devourer come
And eat up my seeds?
Will the enemy triumph over me?
Where do I go from here?
Living a life righteously,
Sometimes falling short of
God's glory—
Do I throw it all away?
Or keep my commitment
And with Jesus stay?

It seems like things are spinning
Out of control.
And I'm tired of feeling like
I'm in a hole,
That the devil's reigning over
My soul—
Laughing, smiling, as he torments me.
My mind,

My flesh,
My spirit
Need peace.

*Peace! Be still!*
I cry out loud,
And when nothing happens
I begin to wonder,
Is this the life God has for me?
Is this a test?
Oh, let it be!

But why do I have to go through it so long?
Why do I have the same sad song?
I feel like a soda bottle shaken up,
Ready to explode!
Or like a fish out of water
When death is trying to take control.
The prince of this world surrounds my soul,
Wrapping my life in a chokehold.

Sometimes I feel like I'm in a maze,
Not knowing which way to go,
Desperately trying to find food for my soul,
Knowing God won't put on me more than I can bear,
But it feels like hell, for this situation hasn't gone anywhere,
So I take it to the Lord in prayer.

God, I need you. Come rescue me!
I need your mighty hand to intervene.
I need you, Lord.
I need you now!
Right now, I request
Your mighty power!
You see, this situation is bigger than I.
The strength of it is stronger than my

*Keyoka Rock*

Natural man can bear.
This issue is so great—my carnal mind
Can't render a solution.
So I turn to you, oh King
For answers—
For guidance.
I turn to you to lead me
Through the surrounding darkness.

For now that I seek you day-to-day,
Now that I worship throughout the day,
The enemy conjures up evil devices and
Sends demonic forces to bombard me with problems.
God, I feel like I'm in a valley
And the shadow of death is haunting me.
I lift my hands to thee.
Please come rescue me!

As I reach to you,
Things become clear.
The atmosphere changes
As your presence draws near.
Your anointing seeps through
My soul,
Filling my cup.
My cup overflows.

You speak peace
In the midst of my storm.
You give me strength
And boldness to stand strong.
Now empowered, I speak
To the enemy of my soul!

Satan, you are a liar, and I bind you now, and
With the help of the Holy Ghost, I tread over your power!
I command your works to return to you void; and
Every evil desire to be destroyed!

I command you to cease your action!
I bind up your plans!
And serve notice—the next time you come against me,
*You will be defeated again*!

# The Unprofitable Enemy

You would think the enemy would stop fighting us
Because God's power resides in us,
But he's just a fool.
Anticipating his tactics would lead to our doom; that's
Quite the contrary—
We can't lose.
In fact, his tactics help in our groom.

Well, it's a blood-born right.
The more the enemy fights
We soar from height to height.
We may become sore in our plight, but
We won't lose sight because
There is no stopping us.
We are victorious, and
Nothing the enemy does
Can keep us bound long enough.

For Jesus breaks every chain,
Cleanses us so we may
Be witnesses to those unaware that
Christ has called their name.

And to those gone astray,
He gave us power to relay
He's married to the backslidden
Seeks those who enjoy sinning.
These souls, we must keep on winning;

Through the power we inherited
From God—the Omnipotent One.
We crush the enemy—the undoubted impotent one.
Intercepting his kingdom has become our resort.
Demonic forces we will seize, and their plans abort;
With God on our side, the enemy always comes up short!

# The Inferno

In the fiery furnace, combating my flesh,
Soul held captive, urges burn—
Passions it wants to express.

I won't bow down to youthful lust,
So I walk in the blaze.
Verbalizing,
Jesus saves!

He is the only God, to whom
I would yield and praise.
I look up, amazed.
Seeing that I'm not alone,
I feel God's power,
Not the heat of the inferno.
God steps down from his throne;
His presence fills my temple.

The rest of the story is quite simple.
I reject sin, so Satan has to flee.
Thanks to God who promised
To strengthen me when I'm weak.

Because of the Blood of the Lamb,
I'm protected—from even me.
My spiritual mind is in control;
My flesh took the back seat.

Embedded in God,
I see no defeat;
Now my mission decrees:
Snatching souls out of darkness
Like Jesus snatched Satan's keys!

# Anointing Activated

1 John 4:7–8 (KJV amplified)

> Beloved, let us love one another, for love is (springs) from God; and he who loves [his fellow men] is begotten (born) of God and is coming [progressively] to know and understand God [to perceive and recognize, getting a better and clearer knowledge of Him]. He who does not love has not become acquainted with God [does not and never did know Him], for God is love.

Ephesians 6: 13 (KJV amplified)

> Therefore, put on God's complete armor, that you may be able to resist and stand your ground on the evil day [of danger], and, having done all [the crisis demands], to stand [firmly in your place].

Luke 10:19 (KJV amplified)

> Behold! I have given you authority and power to trample upon serpents and scorpions, and [physical and mental strength and ability] over all the power that the enemy [possesses]; and nothing shall in any way harm you.

# Saints of God, Pick Up Your Weapons!

We're in the army of the Lord.
Saints of God, pick up your weapons!
The fight is on!
It's time we teach Satan a lesson!

Luke 10:19—
Jesus gave us power
To tread upon serpents, scorpions,
And overall the enemy's power.

Arm yourselves.
Make sure you're prepared.
Ephesians, chapter 6   make sure you have on your gear.
In addition, you must have the spirit of God within you.
So when you come upon the enemy
He won't claim you as being part of his crew.
Carnal Christians, this warning goes out to you too.
How can you defeat the enemy if he's still controlling you?

Saints of God, it's time for us to pick up our weapons.
Denounce those things that are not like God so
We can march on to our blessings.
Just like Christ, we must daily sacrifice our lives
By stripping ourselves from what's wrong
And taking on what is right.

*Keyoka Rock*

Like Michael the Archangel,
We must fight with all our might.
Rebuke the enemy every time he
Comes up in our sight.
Shut down every strategy
Planned for our demise.
If you're scared of the enemy,
Don't even join in this fight.
We need soldiers, ambassadors—
Ready to die for Christ.

Saints of God, it's time for us to pick up our weapons.
It's time we teach Satan a lesson.
If you don't know how to fight in this spiritual battle,
Follow the example of Jehoshaphat and
Those he was connected to.
They sought the Lord—on one accord.
They used weapons of fasting, praying, and worshiping too.
Pleasing the Master, God said, "Hold your peace,
I'll fight for you."

This text found in
2 Chronicles 20 verses 1 through 22
Jehoshaphat and his crew
Approached the battlefield and
Found their enemies had already been killed.
God did it then;
He can do it still.
Together we can defeat the enemy—
Unified, and Holy Spirit–filled.
Saints of God, it's time for us to pick up our weapons.
It's time we teach Satan a lesson.

We can't allow the enemy to turn us against each other.
We must treat one another like true sisters and brothers.
Colossians 3:16—Teach and admonish one another.
Be Christ-led, use wisdom in everything we do—
In the Spirit of love, impart knowledge, wisdom, and truth.

For united we will stand
And divided we will fall.
A house divided against itself can't stand tall.
Saints of God, it's time for us to pick up our weapons.
We must defeat the enemy on every hand, and
March on to our blessings.
We must be the men and the women
God is calling for—strong soldiers in the army of the Lord!

# The Fight Is On! Satan, You're Going Down!

Satan, you think you've won
Just because I fell down.
Prepare to be turned into a clown.
I've got my ephod on; the fight is on now.
Round by round,
I'm sending scripture blows to your crown.
Verbalizing foretold victories,
Blocking out words of the enemy.

I'm in the army of the Lord.
Satan you're going down!
Ephesians 6:13
The armor of God I'm wrapped in now,
Back on my feet, and I'm glad to say that
God called my name, and like Lazarus,
I came back.
Fully equipped—
Blocking punches that you throw at me—
Torments to my mind
By bringing up my history.

Well, I did what you saw,
But I'm not what I've done.
I've been washed in the blood.
Now I'm an heir like God's Son.

You see, I traded filthy rags
For priestly garments instead.
No longer bound—a new life I'm living.
Delivered from the practice and the penalty of sin,
Transformed in my mind, cleansed thoroughly within—
Not just God's creation, but now He calls me *friend*.

Romans 8:1
No condemnation now,
Not looking back at what I've done.
I'm pressing forward now.

My intimacy with God has grown so deep,
When I come into His presence,
"Psalms," He calls me.
Like David, I'm after the heart of the King,
And I won't stop seeking until he comes back for me.

Satan, I see I knocked you off of your feet.
You can't believe you have no more control over me.
Backing away, from God's reflection that you see
As I trample over your power and authority,
I tread upon all devices that you set against me.

There will be no more defeat for me—
Only victory.
Nothing but prosperity is in my destiny.
So the next time you think to make war with me,
Know I'm fully equipped with weaponry.

*Keyoka Rock*

I've got sixty-six books of God's Word, you see.
No device you form will triumph over me.
A defeated foe is all you'll ever be
Every time you think to come against a child of the King!

# God + Issue = Solved

1 Peter 5:7 (KJV amplified)

    Casting the whole of your care [all your anxieties, all your worries, all your concerns, once and for all] on him, for he cares for you affectionately and cares about you watchfully.

Matthew 11:28–30 (KJV amplified)

    Come unto me, all ye that labor and are heavy laden, and I will give you rest. Take my yoke upon you and learn of me; for I am meek and lowly in heart: and ye shall find rest unto your souls. For my yoke is easy, and my burden is light.

# Just a Test

Testing. Testing. Testing.
This is a test of the emergency
Encouraging system.
Please be advised that if you are
Going through any type of trial—
Whether it be on your job
In your home, with friends or family, or
If you're struggling with issues in your mind—
Please note that this is only a test!
Your *going-through* is just part of God's
Making and molding system.
He's building you into a stronger,
Wiser, powerful, and anointed child of God.

Testing. Testing. Testing.
In an event that your troubles begin to
Become too hard for you to bear,
Note that the Lord of hosts,
The Lord mighty in battle
Will be right there.
Please be advised that He will take upon himself
Your heavy load and give you peace.
He will work out your problems when you
Follow these instructions: *trust Him* and *believe Him*.

Remember that the result
Of every trial for a child of God
Is total victory.
This concludes the test
Of the emergency encouraging system.
You may now resume your daily life.

# An "In Spite of" Praise

Life can be long;
Life can be short.
Life can be filled with happiness
And sometimes have a touch of sadness.
Life has its ups and its downs.
In life there is sowing and times of reaping.
There are times of joy and moments of weeping.
No matter what the season you're living in today,
Know that God is with you every step of the way.
During those times when things are going wrong,
Just open your mouth, and on Jesus call.
On those days when things are going just fine,
Look up to heaven and praise the most high.
Whatever the season,
Whatever the test,
Give God your best praise,
And He'll do the rest!

# Tasted Jesus Yet?

Psalm 34:8 (KJV)

> Taste and see that the Lord is good: blessed is the man that trust in him.

Psalm 19:7–11 (NIV)

> The law of the Lord is perfect, reviving the soul. The statues of the Lord are trustworthy, making wise the simple. The precepts of the Lord are right, giving joy to the heart. The commands of the Lord are radiant, giving light to the eyes. The fear of the Lord is pure, enduring forever. The ordinances of the Lord are sure and altogether righteous. They are more precious than gold, than much pure gold; they are sweeter than honey from the comb; By them is your servant warned; in keeping them there is great reward.

# A Love above the Rest

God, your love is so great;
Your love is so free.
Your love wraps all around me,
Especially during times
When things are going wrong.
Your love helps me to overcome.
Your love gives me a victory song.

Like a songbird, I effortlessly sing.
Praises to you, oh God—continuously ring
From my lips of clay, into your tender ears—
Praises that will cause you to draw near.

Thank you for supplying
Your love each and every day;
Because of your love,
I won't stray away from you and stay
In the devil's grip, for your love rescues me.
Love so powerful—it delivers me.

God, your love is above the heavens and
Greater than love displayed on earth.
Your love has me coming back for more.
Lord, please fill my temple;
Let my cup overflow.

Your love is so precious;
Your love is so sweet.
Your love drenches me—like a rainy day.
It drops from the crown of my head
To the soles of my feet.

God, your love is so perfect.
No one can outdo your love,
For it is a beautiful gift,
Which you are the creator of.

# God's Plan of Redemption

God so loved the world,
He gave his only Son
To be crucified on Calvary's cross
For each and every one.

The Son of God, Jesus,
The Lamb who was slain
Took upon the sins of the world
So sinners can be saved.

This redemption plan leads us
To God's will for our lives,
That through our belief in Jesus,
We can obtain eternal life.

# Choose This Day Who You Will Serve

The time is rapidly approaching; Jesus is coming soon.
It may be in the morning, noonday, or midnight hour,
But know He is coming soon.
This message is for adults and young people too.
Get your house in order while you have the time.
For Christ is coming; keep watching the sky.

The Bible notes He's coming like a thief in the night.
For souls who accepted Him as Lord of their life.
Get your house in order while you have the time.
I'm speaking of your physical house, where your soul resides.

Do you know this physical house we're living in
Is not the initial state we were created in?
We were made in the image of God—holy, spotless, righteous—
Until sin entered in.
Now we must be washed in the Blood of the Lamb—Jesus.
He paid the price for our sins.
His sacrificial life enables us life without end and to sit
In heavenly places where there is peace and happiness.

*Keyoka Rock*

Do you know hell was not created for you?
But prepared for Satan and demonic forces
That plan attacks against you.
Do you know, you allow Satan to rule over your life
If you don't allow Jesus to be Lord of your life?

Satan's desire is to steal, kill, and to
Destroy you.
He doesn't want you to obtain
The blessings God has in store for you.
So he blinds your spiritual eyes
And tampers with your flesh,
Causing you to make choices that
Pay wages toward death and damnation.
Hell's pit is what he wants for your demise,
But his death sentence can be reversed
Through your repentance and acceptance of Jesus Christ.

Break the death sentence the enemy planned
For your demise.
Choose life.
Choose Christ,
So when He returns,
It's with Him you can reside.

# References

The King James Version Bible (KJV amplified) and the Thompson Chain Reference Study Bible in the New International Version (NIV) were used in *Petals of the Heart*. Scriptures were cited in some of the poetry written by its author, Keyoka Rock.

### I Fell, but God Picked Me Up!
Romans 7:15–25
St. John 10:10
Isaiah 55:11
2 Corinthians 12:9–10
1 Corinthians 10:13
Ephesians 6:13–18

"And because God is the Greatest Power we shall not be defeated!"—Famous quote by Bishop Hezekiah Walker

### Spiritual Sacrifice: A Desperate Fight to *Live*!
Luke 15:11–24
Romans 7:21–25

### It's Just a Shadow
Psalms 23:4

### Everything Is Going to Be All Right!
Philippians 3:14
Matthew 25:1–13

**Prayer of Distress Births Strength and Victory!**
Luke: 8:5

**The Inferno**
Daniel 3:16–28
James 4:7
Isaiah 40:29
Revelations 1:8

**Saints of God, Pick Up Your Weapons!**
Matthew 12:25

**The Fight Is On!**
**Satan, You're Going Down!**
John 15:15

**Just a Test**
1 Peter 5:7
Matthew 6:33
John 6:35

**An In Spite Of Praise**
Ecclesiastes 3:1–8

**God's Plan of Redemption**
John 3:16

**Choose This Day Who You Will Serve**
John 10:10

Romans 10: 9–10
If you declare with your mouth, "Jesus is Lord," and believe in your heart that God raised him from the dead, you will be saved. For it is with your heart that you believe and are justified, and it is with your mouth that you profess your faith and are saved.
New International Version (NIV)

# About the Author

Keyoka Rock is a Brooklyn, New York, native who has experienced the miraculous power of God in her childhood that changed her life forever. In this book, the author reflects and testifies of her near-death childhood experience and encounter with God that supernaturally resulted in her beating the odds of succumbing to a tragic death, in which she was miraculously awakened from a coma that lasted the duration of seven months, leaving the hospital totally healed from all medical challenges. Her childhood testimony of this miraculous experience helped shape and mold her relationship with God throughout her life, and it has been a personal unshakable attestation to the love and the power of God that has helped her overcome spiritual battles and challenges with her faith in God. These experiences and challenges are poetically expressed in this book and are guaranteed to encourage, empower, and embolden you to trust in the love and power of God "in spite of" what you may be challenged with. In addition to using poetry to uplift and encourage those in despair, Keyoka Rock serves as praise and worship leader and choir director and is a minister of the gospel.

www.ingramcontent.com/pod-product-compliance
Lightning Source LLC
Chambersburg PA
CBHW022357100225
21748CB00035B/315